CW00407302

APPLES

The Musical

IAN DURY

faber and faber
LONDON · BOSTON

First published in 1989
by Faber and Faber Limited
3 Queen Square London WC1N 3AU
in association with the Royal Court Theatre

Photoset by Parker Typesetting Service Leicester
Printed in Great Britain by
Richard Clay Ltd Bungay Suffolk

ISBN 0-571-14349-0

For our mums and dads
from Ian and Mickey

The Royal Court Theatre and Diana Bliss present

APPLES

The Musical

by Ian Dury

Music by Mickey Gallagher

Ian Dury as Byline Browne (*John Haynes*)

CAST LIST

BYLINE BROWNE	Ian Dury
BILLY	Bob Goody
MAGISTRATE	Pam Ferris
SIMPSON	Jesse Birdsall
PC HONEY	Lee Whitlock
DELILAH	Frances Ruffelle
SIR HUGO SINISTER	Alan David
REENIE	Pam Ferris
DEREK	Alan David
LADY WENDY	Pam Ferris
GEORGE	Alan David

Band:

Keyboards	Mickey Gallagher
Bass guitar	Dean Garcia
Saxophone	Davey Payne
Guitar	Merlin Rhys-Jones
Drums	Steve White
Backing Vocals	Dyan Birch
	Frankie Collins
	Paddie McHugh

All other parts played by Members of the Company

There will be one interval

Mickey Gallagher and Ian Dury (*John Haynes*)

Director	Simon Curtis
Choreographer	Anthony Van Laast
Designer	Richard Hudson
Lighting Designer	Nick Chelton
Sound	Ian Horne
	Bryan Bowen
Costume Supervisors	Jennifer Cook
	Cathie Skilbeck
Assistant Director	Anna Birch
Stage Manager	Gemma Bodley
Deputy Stage Manager	Katie Spencer
Assistant Stage Manager	Ali Carron
Student Assistant Stage Manager	Isabel Ashman
Leaflet Design	Sightlines
Production Photographs	John Haynes
Poster	Peter Blake
Graphics	Garden House Press

Wardrobe care by PERSIL and COMFORT, Adhesive by COPYDEX and EVODE LTD, ioniser for the lighting control room by THE LONDON IONISER CENTRE (836 0211), Cordless drill by MAKITA ELECTRIC (UK) LTD, Watches by THE TIMEX CORPORATION, Batteries by EVER READY, Refrigerators by ELECTROLUX and PHILLIPS MAJOR APPLIANCES LTD, Microwave by TOSHIBA UK LTD, Kettles for rehearsals by MORPHY RICHARDS, Video for casting purposes by HITACHI, Cold bottled beer at bar supplied by YOUNG & CO BREWERY, WANDSWORTH. Coffee machines by CONA. Microwave for backstage use kindly supplied by ZANUSSI LTD, Freezer for backstage use supplied by ELECTROLUX "Now that's a good idea". Sound equipment provided by Britannia Row Productions (01 359 0955).

BIOGRAPHIES

JESSE BIRDSALL Theatre includes: *Merry Wives of Windsor, Days of the Commune* (RSC); *Abide with Me* (Contact Theatre, Manchester); *On the Spot!* (Palace Theatre, Watford). Television includes: *A Sudden Wrench, Remembrance, Jangles, Walter, Takes out of School, Annika, We'll Support You, Evermore, Honeymoon, The Fear*. Films include: *Quadrophenia, Bloody Kids, Revolution, Shadey, Wish You Were Here* and *Getting it Right*.

DIANA BLISS Co-producer. Diana was born in Australia and divides her time between Sydney and London. In London, she co-produced *Exclusive Yarns* (Comedy Theatre), a comedy by Stewart Permutt and Gary Lyons; a Bob Sherman comedy, *Big Game*, with Lee Menzies (Nuffield Theatre, Southampton); was Associate Producer for Steven Sewell's *Dreams in an Empty City* (Lyric Hammersmith) and for Arthur Miller's *An Enemy of the People* (Playhouse). Diana is the Australian representative of the Women's Playhouse Trust in London. She produced *Our Country's Good* and *The Recruiting Officer* on tour in Australia with the Royal Court and Sydney Theatre Company, and is delighted to be associated again with the Royal Court on *Apples*.

NICK CHELTON has designed lighting for many plays and musicals in the West End. Most recent designs include *Shirley Valentine, The Wizard of Oz, A Little Night Music*. Designs for opera include: *Rusalka, Doctor Faust, The Magic Flute* (ENO); *The Rake's Progress, Macbeth, Samson and Delila, Un Re in Ascolto* (The Royal Opera); and for most major opera companies throughout Europe and at Houston and Sydney; also work for Kent Opera, Welsh National Opera, Scottish Opera and New Sadlers Wells Opera. Designs for ballet companies include: Ballet Rambert, London Festival Ballet, the Royal Ballet, Sadlers Wells Royal Ballet. Television: *Family*.

SIMON CURTIS Trained at the Royal Court Theatre as Assistant Director to Max Stafford-Clark. Productions at the Royal Court include: *Deadlines* (Joint Stock), *Road, Ourselves Alone, A Lie of the Mind, Greenland*. Other theatre: *Making History, Roots* (National Theatre); *Road* (Lincoln Center/La Mama, New York). Deputy Director at the Royal Court since 1986.

ALAN DAVID For the Royal Court: *Road, The Genius, Panic*. Other theatre includes: *Nicholas Nickelby, As You Like It, Dance of Death* (RSC); *Tale of Two Cities, Dracula* (Liverpool Playhouse); *Oedipus, Twelfth Night* (Oxford Playhouse); *What the Butler Saw* (Belgrade, Coventry); *Destiny* (Half Moon Theatre). Television includes: *Merchant of Venice, Bergerac, Shoestring, Juliet Bravo, Road, The Mountain and the Molehill, The Clinger, Pythons on the Mountain, Hard Cases, Making Out* (second series). Film: *Sakharov*.

IAN DURY For the Royal Court: *Road* and co-writer of songs for *Serious Money*. Other theatre: *Talk of the Devil* (Watford Palace). Television: *King of the Ghetto*. Films include: *The Bearskin; The Cook, the Thief, his Wife and her Lover; The Voice; Burning Beds; Raggedy Rawney; Hearts of Fire; Paradise Unlocked; Rocinante; Pirates* and *Number One*. Solo singer/songwriter and founder member of The Blockheads.

PAM FERRIS For the Royal Court: *Lucky Chance, The Devil's Gateway, The Grace of Mary Traverse*. Other theatre includes: *Roots* (National Theatre); *Exclusive Yarns* (Comedy Theatre); *Having a Ball* (Lyric, Hammersmith); *Nobody's Fool* (Solo Poly); *Cat on a Hot Tin Roof* (Manchester Royal Exchange); *The Cherry Orchard, Women Beware Women* (Oxford Playhouse); *Caucasian Chalk Circle, Country Wife* (Sheffield Crucible). For Shared Experience: *Bleak House, La Ronde, Cymbeline, Arabian Nights, Science Fictions*. Television includes: *Casualty; The Fear; Connie; The Bill; Doger Bonzor and the Rest; Oranges are not the Only Fruit* (to be shown). Films: *Meantime; The House*.

MICKEY GALLAGHER Keyboard player with many notable British bands including The Animals, Skip Bifferty and Heavy Jelly. Has also worked with many other artists including Peter

Frampton, The Clash, Frankie Goes to Hollywood, Eurythmics and Paul McCartney. Was founder member of The Blockheads and co-writer of 'Futures' song in *Serious Money*.

BOB GOODY Theatre includes: *The Arabian Nights Trilogy*, and the one-man play *Insomniac in Morgue Drawer 9* (Shared Experience); *Servant of Two Masters* (Cambridge Theatre Company); *The Black Hole of Calcutta* (National Theatre of Brent); *Hamlet, Comedy of Errors* (RSC Tour); *School for Clowns* (Lillian Bayliss Theatre); with Smith and Goody – co-writer and performer of *'Ave you 'Eard the One about Joey Baker; Irony in Dorking* (Traverse Edinburgh and Kings Head); and *The Gambler* (Hampstead Theatre and the Comedy Theatre). Television includes: *Smith and Goody; Porterhouse Blue; My Family and Other Animals;* co-writer of *Wilderness Road* (BBC comedy series). Films: *Those Glory Glory Days; The Cook, the Thief, his Wife and her Lover*.

RICHARD HUDSON For the Royal Court: *The Emperor*. Other theatre includes: 1988 season at the Old Vic (winner of the Laurence Olivier Award and Critics' Drama Award as Best Designer) for *Andromache, One Way Pendulum, Bussy D'Ambois, The Tempest, Too Clever by Half*; also designed *King Lear* (Old Vic); *The Misanthrope* (National Theatre); The Master Builder (RSC); *Don Carlos* (Royal Exchange, Manchester). Opera designs include: *A Night at the Chinese Opera* (Kent Opera); *Manon* (RNCM and Opera North); *Mignon* (Wexford Festival); *La Vie Parisienne* (Scottish Opera); *Don Pasquale* (Opera Northern Ireland); *Count Ory* (Kent Opera); *Candide* (Scottish Opera and Old Vic).

FRANCES RUFFELLE Theatre includes: *The Sleeping Prince* (Chichester Festival Theatre and Theatre Royal Haymarket); *Starlight Express* (Apollo Victoria); *Les Misérables* (RSC Barbican, Palace Theatre and Broadway Theatre, New York) for which she won a Tony Award, Helen Hayes Award, Theatre World, Outer Critics Circle Award. Television includes: *P'Tang Yang Kipperbang; Marks; S.W.A.L.K.; Tucker's Luck; The Equalizer*.

LEE WHITLOCK Theatre includes: *The Best Years of Your Life* (Man in the Moon); *Gregory's Girl* (Crucible Theatre). Television includes: *The Merry Wives of Windsor; The Gentle Touch; Cribb; Shine on Harvey Moon; Hold the Back Page; The Best Years of Your Life; Mates; Me and My Girl; Starting Out; Split Ends; The Two of Us*. Films: *The Mirror Crack'd; Wish You Were Here*.

ANTHONY VAN LAAST Choreography for theatre includes: *Song and Dance* (Palace Theatre); *Blondel* (Old Vic/Aldwych); *Annie Get Your Gun* (Chichester and Aldwych): *Peter Pan* (Aldwych/Cambridge); *A Little Night Music* (Chichester/Piccadilly); *Pirates of Penzance* (Savoy); *Candide* (Scottish Opera/Old Vic); *Mikado* (ENO); *Peer Gynt, The Merry Wives of Windsor, A Midsummer Night's Dream, Romeo and Juliet* (RSC). Television includes: *The Hot Shoe Show; Bluebell;* Royal Variety performances; *A Midsummer Marriage*. Films include: *Excalibur; Outlaws; Who Dares Wins; Nutcracker; Never Say Never Again; Hope and Glory*.

A BRIEF HISTORY OF THE ENGLISH STAGE COMPANY AT THE ROYAL COURT

The English Stage Company was formed in 1956 to bring serious writing back to the stage. The aim was that writers should explore subjects drawn from contemporary life and that the plays that were produced would be challenging and innovatory as well as of the highest quality. With only the second production the company struck gold: John Osborne's *Look Back in Anger* is the play that has been credited with propelling British theatre into the modern age. Since then the English Stage Company has never looked back. As well as reviving often neglected classics, it has premièred the work of playwrights who are now performed the world over, attracting stars such as Olivier, Richardson, Gielgud and Ashcroft into new plays by writers such as John Osborne, David Storey, Edward Bond, Arnold Wesker and Ann Jellicoe.

The line continued with writers such as David Hare and Howard Brenton. Both were first produced at the Royal Court early on in their careers. More recently, Caryl Churchill has reached a wide audience after early beginnings in the Theatre Upstairs and writers such as Timberlake Wertenbaker, Hanif Kureishi, Jim Cartwright and Anne Devlin have had work produced. Recent critical and box office successes have included *Top Girls, Serious Money, Road, Tom and Viv, Insignificance* and *Our Country's Good*.

After thirty-three years, the Royal Court Theatre is still the most important forum in Britain for the production of new work. Scores of plays first seen in Sloane Square have become part of the national and international dramatic repertoire. It is now the only theatre with a main stage that is consistently producing new work and although funding shortages mean that it can only function on an occasional basis, the Theatre Upstairs remains one of the most significant studio theatres in the country.

As a place where reputations are made, and as a bridgehead to other areas of the profession and to film and television, the Royal Court's contribution to British theatre is incalculable.

ROYAL COURT THEATRE
THE RECRUITING
OFFICER
BY GEORGE FARQUHAR
AND
OUR COUNTRY'S
GOOD
THE ENGLISH STAGE COMPANY AT THE ROYAL COURT

THE ROYAL COURT THEATRE SOCIETY

For many years now Members of the Royal Court Theatre Society have received special notice of new productions, but why not become a Friend, Associate or a Patron of the Royal Court, thereby involving yourself directly in maintaining the high standard and unique quality of Royal Court productions – while enjoying complimentary tickets to the shows themselves? Subscriptions run for one year; to become a Member costs £10, a Friend £50 (joint)/£35 (single), an Associate £350, a Patron £1,000.

PATRONS

Jeffrey Archer, Diana Bliss, Caryl Churchill, Issac Davidov, Alfred Davis, Mr & Mrs Nicholas Egon, Mrs Henny Gestetner, Lady Eileen Joseph, Henry Kaye, Tracey Ullman, Julian Wadham.

ASSOCIATES

Peter Boizot, David Capelli, Michael Codron, Jeremy Conway, Stephen Fry, Elizabeth Garvie, The Earl of Gowrie, David Hart, London Arts Discovery Tours, Patricia Marmont, Barbara Minto, Greville Poke, Michael Serlin, Sir Dermont de Trafford, Nick Hern Books, Richard Wilson.

FRIENDS

Paul Adams, Roger Allam & Susan Todd, Robin Anderson, Jane Annakin, John Arthur, Mrs M. Bagust, Martine Baker, Dee Barnfield, Linda Bassett, Paul Bater, Josephine Beddoe, Laura Birkett, Anthony Blond, Bob Boas, Irving H. Brecker, Katie Bradford, Jim Broadbent, Alan Brodie, Ralph Brown, A. J. H. Buckley, Stuart Burge, Neil Goodhue Cady, Laurence Cann, Susan Card, Guy Chapman, Steve Childs, Ruby Cohn,Angela Coles, Sandra Cook, Lynn & Bernhard Cottrell, Lou Coulson, Peter Cregeen, Harriet Cruickshank, B. R. Cuzner, Mrs Der Pao Graham, Anne Devlin, Mrs V. A. Dimant, Julia Dos Santos, R. H. & B. H. Dowler, Adrian Charles Dunbar, Susan Dunnett, Pamela Edwardes, George A. Elliott III, Jan Evans, Trevor Eve, Kenneth Ewing, Leonard Fenton, Mr & Mrs Thomas Fenton, Kate Feast, M. H. Flash, Robert Fox, Gilly Fraser, David Gant, Kerry Gardner, Anne Garwood, Sarah Garner, Alfred Molina & Jill Gascoine, Jonathan Gems, Frank & Woji Gero, Beth Goddard, Lord Goodman, Joan Grahame, Roger Graef, Rod Hall, Sharon Hamper, Shahab Hanif, A. M. Harrison, Vivien Heilbron, Jan Harvey, Peter Headill, Sarah Hellings, Jocelyn Herbert, Ashley & Pauline Hill, David Horovitch, Dusty Hughes, Vi Hughes, Diana Hull, Susan Imhof, Trevor Ingman, Kenny Ireland, Jonathan Isaacs, Alison E. Jackson, Richard Jackson, Dick Jarrett, B. E. Jenkins, Hugh Jenkins, Dominic Jephcott, Paul Jesson, Donald Jones, Dr & Mrs David Josefowitz, Annely Juda, Elizabeth Karr Tashman, Sharon Kean, Alice Kennelly, Jean Knox, Sir Kerry & Lady St. Johnston, Mrs O. Lahr, Dr R. J. Lande, Iain Lanyon, Hugh Laurie, Alison Leathart, Peter Ledeboer, C. C. Lee, Sheila Lemon, Peter L. Levy, Robert S. Linton, Mr & Mrs M. M. Littman, Roger & Moira Lubbock, John & Erica Macdonald, Suzie Mackenzie, Marina Mahler, Paul Mari, Rosy Nasreen & Dr Conal Liam Mannion, Marina Martin, Patricia Marx, Anna Massey, S. A. Mason, Paul Matthews, Elaine Maycock, Phillip L. McDonald, Ian McMillan, James Midgley, Louise Miller, Anthony Minghella, L. A. G. Morris, T. Murnaghan, Alex Nash, Linda Newns, Sally Newton, John

Nicholls, Michael Nyman, Nick Marston, Richard O'Brien, Eileen & John O'Keefe, Donald O'Leary, P. O'Shea, Stephen Oliver, Gary Olsen, Mark Padmore, Norman Papp, Alan David & Jane Penrose, Pamela Percy, Ronald Pickup, Pauline Pinder, Harold Pinter, Nigel Planer, Laura Plumb, Peter Polkinghorne, Dr A. G. Poulsen Hansen, Trevor Preston, Dr G. Pullen and Mrs P. Black, R. Puttick, Margaret Ramsay, Jane Rayne, B. J. & Rosmarie Reynolds, E. W. Richards, Alan Rickman, David Robb, Martin & Jennifer Roddy, R. S. Rubin, Christie Ryan, George Scheider, Rosemary Squire, A. J. Sayers, Leah Schmidt, Martin & Glynis Scurr, Jennifer Sebag-Montefiore, Mrs L. M. Sieff, Paul Sinclair Brooke, Andrew Sinclair and Sonia Melchett, Ms. A. M. Jamieson & Mr A. P. Smith, Peter A. Smith, Jane Snowden, Max Stafford-Clark, Ms Caroline Staunton, Louise Stein, Jenny Stein, Jeff Steitzer,Lindsay Stevens, Pearl Stewart, Richard Stokes, Richard Stone, Rob Sutherland, Dudley Sutton, Audrey & Gordon Taylor, Steve Tedbury, Nigel Terry, Mary Trevelyan, Amanda and R. L. W. Triggs, Elizabeth Troop, Mrs Anne Underwood, Kiomars Vejdani, Maureen Vincent, Karen and Wes Wadman, Andrew Wadsworth, Harriet Waiter, Julie Walters, Tim Watson, Nicholas Wright, Charles & Victoria Wright.

Laurence Olivier 1907–1989
(*Snowdon*)

THE OLIVIER APPEAL

The Royal Court Theatre was very proud of Lord Olivier's patronage of our Appeal. It will continue in his name as a memorial to his life and talent.
The Appeal was launched in June 1988 – the Royal Court's 100th anniversary year. The target is £800,000 to repair and refurbish the theatre and to enable the English Stage Company to maintain and continue its worldwide reputation as Britain's 'National Theatre of new writing'. The Royal Court would like to thank the following for their generous contributions to the Appeal:

Adwest Group plc
Jeffrey Archer
Edgar Astaire
Associated British Foods
Andrew Bainbridge
The Clifford Barclay Trust
Phyllis Blackburn
The Elaine and Neville Blond Charitable Trust
Paul Brooke
Isador Caplan
Peter Carter
Geoffrey Chater
Graham Cowley
David Crosner
The Douglas Heath Eves Trust
Douglas Fairbanks
The Economist
The Esmee Fairbairn Trust
Esselte Letraset
Matthew Evans
Evans and Reiss
Robert Fleming Bank
D J Freeman & Company
Brian Friel
Michael Frayn
Gala (100th Anniversary)
The Godinton Trust
Caroline Goodall
Lord Goodman
Roger Graef
Christopher Hampton
Hatter (IMO) Foundation
The Hedley Trust
Claude Hug
Mr and Mrs Trevor John
The John Lewis Partnership
The Kobler Trust
The London and Edinburgh Trust
The Mercers
National Westminster Bank
Anna Louise Neuberg Trust
Olivier Banquet
A. J. G. Patenall
Pirelli Ltd
A. J. R. Purssell
Mr and Mrs J. A. Pye's Charitable Settlement
St Quentin Ltd
The Rayne Foundation
R. S. Rubin
The Lord Sainsbury Trust
Save & Prosper Group
Paul Schofield
Andrew Sinclair
D. R. Slack
W. H. Smith & Son
The Spencer-Wills Trust
Max Stafford-Clark
'Stormy Monday' Charity Première
Mary Trevelyan
Andrew Wadsworth
Women's Playhouse Trust
Sandra Yarwood

FOR THE ROYAL COURT

DIRECTION

Artistic Director	Max Stafford-Clark
Deputy Director	Simon Curtis
Casting Director	Lisa Makin
Literary Manager	Kate Harwood
Assistant Director	Philip Howard
Artistic Assistant	Melanie Kenyon
Arts Council Writer in Residence	Clare McIntyre
Gerald Chapman Award Trainee Director	Anna Birch

PRODUCTION

Production Manager	Bo Barton
Chief Electrician	Colin Roxborough
Deputy Chief Electrician	James Armstrong
Electrician	Denis O'Hare*
Sound Designer	Bryan Bowen
Board Operators	Jonquil Pantin,* Steve Hepworth*
Master Carpenter	Chris Bagust
Deputy Master Carpenter	Alan Joyce
Technical Manager, Theatre Upstairs	Stephen Munn
Wardrobe Supervisor	Jennifer Cook
Deputy Wardrobe Supervisor	Cathie Skilbeck
Wardrobe Assistant	Sam McAling

ADMINISTRATION

General Manager	Graham Cowley
Assistant to General Manager	Georgia Cheales
Finance Administrator	Mark Rubenstein
Finance Assistant	Rachel Harrison
Press (730 2652)	Tamsin Thomas
Marketing & Publicity Manager	Guy Chapman
Development Manager	Anne-Marie Thompson
Development Assistant	Jacqueline Vieira
House Manager	William Day
Deputy House Manager	Alison Smith
Bookshop	Angela Toulmin-Hunt*
Box Office Manager	Gill Russell
Box Office Assistants	Gerald Brooking, Rita Sharma
Stage Door/Telephonists	Angela Toulmin-Hunt, Jan Noyce*
Evening Stage Door	Tyrone Lucas*
Maintenance	John Lorrigio
Cleaners	Eileen Chapman*, Ivy Jones*
Firemen	Paul Kleinmann*, David Wyatt*

YOUNG PEOPLE'S THEATRE

Director	Elyse Dodgson
Administrator	Dominic Tickell
Youth and Community Worker	Euton Daly

*Part-time staff

This Theatre is associated with the Regional Theatre Young Directors' Scheme.

ACT ONE

The DRUNKEN BUSKER *is chased on stage and the* CHORUS *begins 'You Are Here'.*

'You Are Here'

CHORUS:

Smile as you enter the theatre, ticket in hot little hand
Glad that you forked out a tenner, the view from the circle is grand
Smirk at the state of the patrons, can this be the cream of Sloane Square?
Clutching your programme and poppets, sit down and pretend you're not
There goes drinkers' last warning; time for a triple or two
Do place interval orders; or risk an incredible queue
Save your discussions till after, try not to cough out of time
Our staff have just bolted the toilets; hang on to your lager and lime

You are here: providing your amusement is our major task
You are here: complicity is all we ask.

(*We see* DELILAH *lifting a large black briefcase and putting items into her bag. The* SINISTER MINISTER *appears, steaming hot in his bath robe, and dresses in his ministerial suit, leaving the trouser-leg rolled up. They exit.*)

The scene is a courtroom in London, the time starts six months ago
The hero's a bit of a villain, the heroine's an equity pro
In craving your further indulgence, you will make an effort, I know
If you'll please sing along with each chorus, we'll all have a jolly good show

You are here: providing our amusement is your major task
You are here: complicity is all we ask
You are here: you are here: you are here: you are here

We see the courtroom. BYLINE *and* BILLY *are outside Court Number 2.*

BYLINE BROWNE: (*Into vodaphone*) Yes, yes, of course it's big. I've pulled out all the stops on this one. Look, I need a few more days, OK? Did you get the smudges back yet? How's the detail?

BILLY: (*Produces photo and gives it to* BYLINE) She's got lovely legs but you can't see his face. Jonesy says he's sorry but without a flash the old telephoto always gets a bit murky.

BYLINE BROWNE: (*Pockets the photo*) How did you find out she was here today? You don't go round looking at the lists, do you?

BILLY: She came up on my computer: possible conspiracy charge, but very hard to prove. I'll go and have a look. She'll be on in a minute; that squeak in the grey suit is her brief. (BILLY *goes into the courtroom.* BYLINE *addresses the audience.*)

BYLINE BROWNE: I'm a reporter. I make an excuse and stay on the case. I pay people good money to tell me they fucked a spaceman. I've had more doorsteps than hot dinners.

BILLY: (*Returns from Court Number 2*) She'll be all right, he's a bleeding queen's. You don't see a lot of them down here.

BYLINE BROWNE: Is she going to be referred with the rest of 'em?

BILLY: No, she'll be out in half an hour. (*He goes back in.*)

BYLINE BROWNE: I am yardstick, masthead and bastion of all things errant or tragic in or out of the public domain. I am that viper.

BILLY: (*Returns from Court Number 2*) You are that viper.

BYLINE BROWNE: You know my work and subsidize my revelations. This is my song:

'Byline Browne'

I'm here to find out what makes you tick
I'm here to discover the secret you
I intend to reveal that you're crooked and sick
And I DON'T give a damn if none of it's true

Cos I'm Byline Browne from the national press
And that is how I earn my wages
I bring exposure and distress
As I spread your guts across the centre pages

I'm here to solicit your innermost thoughts
I'm fuelled by jealousy, venom and drink
I poke in your dustbins and I lurk round the courts
And I puke up your portrait in bright yellow ink

Cos I'm Byline Browne of the popular press
The man who brought you babies for sale
I'll blackmail your neighbour and look up your dress
But come what may, I'll tell my tale

I cover each item as issues arise
With a skein of fabric of tissue of lies
I'll fuck up your family, your future and friends
And I'll see you in hell before my story ends

I'm a reporter with senses and hunches
Somebody's daughter's turned into a junkie
I'm on a reporter's expenses and lunches
And a whisky and water and I don't give a monkeys

Get the picture? Yes, we see

BILLY: Are you a bimbo?
BYLINE BROWNE: I'm on a story. I'm hunting a snake in high places. The Sinister Minister. Go and check our witness.

BILLY: (*With mock subservience*) I'll go and check our witness. (*He leaves.*)

BYLINE BROWNE: Sir Hugo Sinister: he's the one I'm after. I've hated this bastard since I was doing funerals in Luton. That's when I first heard the whispers about the boy in the mask. His rise through the ranks; his automatic assumption of grace and favour are widely and quietly known to be directly related to his pre-eminence in the secret world of ritualized depravity. His vice and blackmail ring extends beyond government into industry, and by exposing it I will not only destroy his power base, but I'll make the Blotsky scandal look like Babes in the Wood. It will be the crowning achievement of my career and I'll earn enough money to be able to stop doing this horrible fucking job.

BILLY: (*Sticking his head out*) She'll be on soon.

BYLINE BROWNE: I am going to get him! (*He spits.*)

We enter the court and 'The Courtroom Song' begins. BYLINE *sings from the wings.*

'The Courtroom Song'

BYLINE:

What have we got on today?
One stealing and taking away
Is there anything you wish to say?
You'll go down for a year and a day
Down for a year and a day
Down for a year and a day

(*The* DRUNKEN BUSKER *is led into the dock.*)

MAGISTRATE: I'm putting you down as of no fixed address. I can't believe you live at number 70 Regent Street. I want you to make contact with your welfare officer in Lambeth as soon as possible. Do you understand?

(*The* DRUNKEN BUSKER *shuffles in the affirmative.*)

Prison is not the proper place for you, but you cannot be allowed to scream and spit at passers-by who refuse to give you money. Do you have anything to say?

DRUNKEN BUSKER: I believe probably that I am guilty.

MAGISTRATE: £25 or one day for harassment, alarm and distress. Do you understand?

(*We hear another chorus of 'The Courtroom Song'.* SIMPSON *is in the dock.*)

BYLINE:

You were caught robbing Dickins & Jones
Though you say you were working alone
You were linked on a radio phone
To a van in a no-parking zone
A van in a no-parking zone
A van in a no-parking zone

MAGISTRATE: This is the third time you've been before me this year, Mr Simpson. Business must be good.

SIMPSON: Mustn't grumble Mrs Harris, how's the family?

MAGISTRATE: Very well, thank you. Fined £30 for obstructing the pavement, £50 for illicit trading.

(SIMPSON *leaves and* PC HONEY *steps forward to address* MAGISTRATE. *He removes his notebook from his uniform jacket pocket and clears his throat.*)

PC HONEY: With your permission, ma'am, I have to inform the court that the defendant standing in the dock, charged under the name of Josephine McKenzie on one count of insulting behaviour likely to cause a breach of the peace, two counts of indecent assault, and fourteen counts of persistent aggravated public nuisance contrary to paragraphs 97, 93 and 47 of the public order act of 1969, is in actual fact a male person, one Arthur George Wallace, labourer, of no permanent address, currently resident at the social services hostel in Vauxhall, otherwise known as the marmite factory. At 8.45 last night, the evening of the third of April, myself, PC Honey 739, stationed at Kennington police station, was on street patrol duty in the vicinity of Waterloo station when I received a call on my personal receiver to proceed to the area of platform 19 on the main concourse, where a woman had been reported creating a serious disturbance at the entrance to the gentlemen's lavatories. I arrived at 8.53 and took up a concealed position behind the Datsun car display opposite platforms 16 and 17. From 8.54 until 9.32 I observed the defendant's behaviour. He was wearing the same headscarf and camelhair coat, and carrying the same leather handbag that he is now, and I observed his making advances of a lewd and suggestive nature on seventeen separate occasions to male travellers entering the gents about their lawful business, on at least two of which occasions he made actual physical contact with the said male traveller's person, the second of which caused an immediate affray upon which I left my place of concealment, and proceeded to caution and subsequently arrest the defendant Wallace. At the time of arrest I did not realize that the defendant Wallace was a male person, and before giving him into the charge of WPC Jones of Kennington police station, I asked him to account for his unusual behaviour. 'You wouldn't understand Constable,' he said; 'it's me change.'

(*We hear chorus of 'The Courtroom Song'.* DELILAH *is in the dock.*)

BYLINE:

You were found with a kilo of hash
Which you claim was your personal stash
Since your pockets were bulging with cash
Your statement is pure balderdash
Your statement is pure balderdash
Your statement is pure balderdash

MAGISTRATE: Delilah Dolittle, although you admit to having intimate relations with all three defendants, you claim to have had no knowledge whatsoever about their proposed crime. Since you state under oath that you had no idea that the three Victorian pendants found in your possession at 43B Chalfont Mews were part of the proceeds of the said robbery, I have no alternative but to sentence you to six months for accessory after the fact, and six months concurrent for possession of stolen goods suspended for two years. Do you understand?

DELILAH: (*Glad to get a result*) Thank you very much, your honour.
(*We hear final chorus of 'The Courtroom Song'*.)

BYLINE:

I can hardly believe what I hear
You swear you were able to steer
That your vision and speech were quite clear
And you'd only had twelve pints of beer
Only had twelve pints of beer
Only had twelve pints of beer

DELILAH *leaves Court Number 2 and* BYLINE BROWNE *stops her*.

BYLINE BROWNE: Excuse me, may I call you Miss? I'm with DPI: Disgusting Press International.

DELILAH: Well, piss off, then.

BYLINE BROWNE: Hold up, lassie, I'm not after you or your three boyfriends. It's bigger fish I seek. Tell me about the Wagmore Club.

DELILAH: (*Very scared suddenly*) Oh my God. We can't talk here.

BYLINE BROWNE: (*Reassuringly*) Come along, my dear, I know a nice quiet pub.

The Sinister Minister's office. We hear a snatch of 'The Sinister Minister Theme'.

SINISTER MINISTER: (*He is frantically searching his big black briefcase*) Have you been organizing my pouch, Mrs Latymer?

REENIE: (*With fifteen years of mild disdain*) No Minister, since you've not been here these past two ticks, I haven't had the time. What are you looking for? The minutes of the select committee?

SINISTER MINISTER: (*To himself*) No, the minutes of the Wagmore Club.
(*To* REENIE) A bulging manila folder, a small black notebook, and sundry videotapes and floppy discs, all stamped top secret and sealed by privy. I normally keep them in Dolphin Square.

REENIE: (*Bored rigid by his pranky lifestyle*) Sir, it is my place to deal only with your affairs of state.

SINISTER MINISTER: Mine aren't the only mucky fingers,

Latymer. Heads might roll and crowns be set a-tremble.

REENIE: And not for the last time, I'm sure.

SINISTER MINISTER: This material would topple HMG if it fell into the wrong hands. *Reenie*, please help me, I'm nearly on my knees.

REENIE: You would have swapped me for a moist young débutante years ago if I didn't know so much about you. Why should I help you?

SINISTER MINISTER: Does your incorruptibility stem merely from limited horizons or is there an unseen string to your bow?

REENIE: If you have to ask that question, you'll never know the answer.

(*'The Sinister Minister Theme' begins.*)

'The Sinister Minister Theme'

REENIE: (*Looking at his back; he's gazing ahead*)

There's been some times these fifteen years
When I would have gladly relished
Dropping you from fifteen floors
Into the shit
But now my main concern lies solely
With the far less guilty mortals
Or the innocent passers-by
That you might hit

SINISTER MINISTER: (*Almost ready for emergency plan; excited*)

Yes, God help those I leave behind
If this gets out, I've made a plan
To fool the world into thinking
That I'm dead
And I'll be off to Paraguay
I'll strew my clothes along the beach
And leave my car on top of Beachy Head

REENIE: (*She doesn't blame him for his evilness*)

Corrupted in the cradle though you were by darker forces
Still your truth to form astounds me
None the less

There's not much time, you wretched swine
To find your missing minutes
We've already had inquiries
From the press

SINISTER MINISTER: (*Like a fox he can instantly refocus*)

I spent the night in Lady Wendy's
Rumpus room astride a
Little filly that I picked up
at the club . . . Giddy up
I leave the combination to my
Briefcase on my watchstrap
I suppose she had the time while I was in my tub . . . rub a dub dub, change baskets.

REENIE:

Corrupted in the cradle though you were
By darker forces
Your truth to form astounds me
None the less
I'd love to see you swing for all your crimes
But there are far too many
Other people caught up
In this mess

SINISTER MINISTER:

So should I fly to Paraguay
Having strewn my clothes along the beach
And left my car on top of Beachy Head?
Or is there time to track her down
Retrieve the stolen documents
And silence her before the story's spread?

REENIE:

Other people caught up in this mess

SINISTER MINISTER:

Silence her before the story's spread

REENIE:

Other people caught up in this mess

SINISTER MINISTER:

Silence her before the story's spread

REENIE: Have you spoken to your filthy sister?

(*They exit opposite ways still singing the last repeated lines.*)

BYLINE BROWNE *and* DELILAH *in the pub. They have drinks: VAT and GAT. Lemons float.*

BYLINE BROWNE: Right, first off, nothing's going to come down on you. I give you my word.

DELILAH: Bollocks!

BYLINE BROWNE: (*He drinks*) You know who I'm after, don't you?

You were seen coming out of the Wagmore with him only last night.

(*Shows her the photo.*)

DELILAH: This thing is bigger than both of us, sweetheart. Somebody might cut out heads off.

BYLINE BROWNE: That doesn't happen over here, as well you know. Christine's still ticking over, isn't she?

This is a big story. (*He produces a chequebook.*) I'm talking area codes. When it's as big as this, it's like the Abbey National. My paper will not only guarantee your complete safety but will underwrite your financial security in the fugitive society of your choice, and believe me, there are some bloody good ones.

DELILAH: I'm just a working person. What could I know?

BYLINE BROWNE: I want his ministerial knickers hanging from a tree. To my knowledge, you've been putting yourself about with the gentry for at least five years. You know all the names and all the places. You were one of the original whippogram girls before you became a Wagmore sufferagette. All I need to nail Sir Hugo Sinister is your sworn affidavit that he is the organizer and procurer behind this evil vice ring that has permeated the highest reaches of our society.

DELILAH: Do me a favour. You love it. You're on a jolly-up. Bollocks to our society! You're just another brass yourself.

BYLINE BROWNE: And we both stand to get a bloody good earner out of it, lassie. Now come on. What do you say?

DELILAH: I'll have to think about it, sweetheart.

BILLY *and* SIMPSON *set up the stall and recite 'The Bus Drivers' Prayer'.*

SIMPSON: Our father who art in Hendon
BILLY: Harrow Road by thy name
SIMPSON: Thy Kingston come
BILLY: Thy Wimbledon
TOGETHER: In Erith as it is in Hendon
SIMPSON: Give us this day our Berkhamsted
BILLY: And forgive us our Westminsters
TOGETHER: As we forgive those who Westminster against us
SIMPSON: And lead us not into Temple station
BILLY: But deliver us from Ealing
SIMPSON: For thine is the Kingston
BILLY: The Purley and the Crawley
SIMPSON: For Iver
BILLY: and Iver
TOGETHER: Crouch End

SIMPSON: (*Still setting up his stall*) Are you getting enough? Come on, girls. Come and get your Piccadilly comforters. More for the pound all round. Fresh in today the strawberries! If I don't get an edge, I won't get no wedge.

BILLY: How's the classes going?

SIMPSON: I'll be honest with you, since I've been earning an honest crust I've been too bloody knackered to get it together. I've lapsed me English and me History, but I'm still doing the Life Drawing cos she's half a sort. Sixty pence a pound your button mush!

BILLY: Self is the narrowest angle between any two horizons.

SIMPSON: You didn't read that in the *Bugle*. How's the dodgy parson trade?

BILLY: Browney thinks he's on a big one. We might be nipping over to Marbella.

SIMPSON: I wouldn't mind a bit of that myself. Come and get your ripe and lovely apples! What did you think of that Eric Ambler book?

BILLY: I think it's his best work since the Levanter. He's a good-looking bastard as well.

SIMPSON: (*Rapid-fire verbal*) I've just been for a short walk in the Hindu Kush.

BILLY: (*Equally rapid*) I'm on a slow boat to China

SIMPSON: (*Languorously*) I love the lady in the lake

BILLY: (*Upfully*) I've fallen upon hard times

SIMPSON: That's what I'd really like to be. A writer. Instead of a nobody, which is what I am.

BILLY: I could write a book as the ageing Sidney Falco, but it wouldn't half be boring.

SIMPSON: D'you ever regret giving up thieving?

BILLY: Not even when it's raining.

(*The 'Apples' theme begins and* DELILAH *appears.*)

'Apples'

Delilah the dancer from Soho, was making her way down the lane
Simpson from Harrow had fruit on barrow, he sold it for love and for gain
Simpson said, 'Hello young woman, my pippins are lovely today
Don't be suspicious of golden delicious, whatever your granny might say

'They're only apples, red and green
Apples, lovely, ripe and juicy and especially for you
Right off my barrow, my old cock sparrow
Apples, red and green'

Delilah the dancer from Soho, took ages to make up her mind
Simpson said, 'Madam, you'd know if you'd had them that these are the very best kind
This is the pick of the orchard, forgive me a figure of speech
But apples like these here just don't grow on trees dear and this one is really a peach

'They're only apples, red and green
Apples, lovely ripe and juicy and especially for you
Right off my barrow, my old cock sparrow
Apples, red and green'

Simpson picked out a green apple, he polished it up on
his sleeve
He said, 'Do me a favour and savour the flavour of what
you're about to receive'
Delilah the dancer from Soho, accepted his gift with a
smile
She said, 'It looks like a good 'un, it'll do for my pudden
I'll get round to it after a while'

'They're only apples, red and green
Apples, lovely ripe and juicy and especially for you
Right off my barrow, my old cock sparrow
Apples, red and green.'

(As the song ends they have a little kiss.)
*(*SIMPSON *fancies his chances with* DELILAH *and they both sing 'Love is All'.)*

'Love is All'

SIMPSON:
When ecstasy enobled our first kiss
I fell into an agony of bliss
DELILAH:
I've never heard a person talk like this
I hope you don't think you can take the piss
SIMPSON:
The exhilarating rapture of your touch
Ensnares my heart within its vice-like clutch
DELILAH:
Though that may be a compliment as such
I'm not sure that I like it very much

SIMPSON:

Come to my arms

DELILAH:

So put your hands

SIMPSON:

Oh cherished love

DELILAH:

Where they belong

SIMPSON:

As spirits soar

DELILAH:

Although it's cruel

SIMPSON:

To worlds above

DELILAH:

You must be strong

SIMPSON:

And while we pledge

DELILAH:

Stop talking horse shit

SIMPSON:

Our hearts be true

DELILAH:

In my ear

SIMPSON:

This perfect dream

DELILAH:

You're not my cup

SIMPSON:

Of me and you

DELILAH:

Of tea, I fear

SIMPSON:

Cos love is all

DELILAH:

Oh no it ain't

SIMPSON:

Yes, love is all

The sweet unbridled urges you evoke
My fevered brow is bursting till I choke

DELILAH:

Although you seem to think you're quite a bloke
I wouldn't want you even for a joke

SIMPSON:

Come to my arms

DELILAH:

So put your hands

SIMPSON:

Oh cherished love

DELILAH:

Where they belong

SIMPSON:

As spirits soar

DELILAH:

Although it's cruel

SIMPSON:

To worlds above

DELILAH:

You must be strong

SIMPSON:

And while we pledge

DELILAH:

Stop talking bollocks

SIMPSON:

Our hearts be true

DELILAH:

In my ear

SIMPSON:

This perfect dream

DELILAH:

You're not my cup

SIMPSON:

Of me and you

DELILAH:

Of tea, I fear

SIMPSON:

Cos love is all

DELILAH:

Oh no it ain't

SIMPSON:

Yes, love is all

DELILAH:

Oh no it ain't

SIMPSON:

Love is all

DELILAH:

Oh no it ain't

SIMPSON:

Love is all

BYLINE *and* BILLY *are in the street.*

BILLY: Was that a blank, or what?

BYLINE BROWNE: I think she might be on the bubble. (*He gets out his notebook.*) Who else do we know about?

BILLY: Jonesy got Lord Blue-tit last night clear as a bell, with the Santisi sisters, coming out of the Chelsea Rotter, and guess where they were going?

BYLINE BROWNE: Stringwalls? I don't bloody know.

BILLY: Round her house for a knees-up: Lady Wendy Brompton-Cocktail Sinister.

BYLINE BROWNE: His bloody sister!

BILLY: Very true.

BYLINE BROWNE: I'm on my way. 10–4.

The CHORUS *sings 'Still Waters', and* LADY WENDY *and* DEREK *sing 'Another Dark Day for Derek'.*

'Still Waters'

CHORUS:

Don't trouble the water
Leave it alone
Why don't you

Why don't you
Let it be?
Still waters run deep
Yes they do
Oh, yeah, yeah.

'Another Dark Day for Derek'

LADY WENDY:

'Twas another dark day for Derek, 'tis a miracle that he survived
He'd split up with Joan, they'd cut off his phone
And his giro still hadn't arrived
So he walked to the Chelsea Embankment, intent on a watery sleep
Got up on a ledge, looked over the edge
And got himself ready to leap

CHORUS:

Oy vay, another rotten day, it's hard to be alive
Hey hey, don't throw yourself away, Derek, please don't dive

DEREK:

Lady Wendy, who should have know better, who'd squandered her assets on vice
Awoke very late in a god-awful state
Determined to flee paradise
She got a cab to the Chelsea Embankment and plunged fully clad into the drink

LADY WENDY:

As did Derek, poor sod, thinking he was on his tod

DEREK *and* LADY WENDY:

And both rapidly started to sink.

CHORUS:

Oh dear, we watch them disappear, into the murky Thames
We fear the end is very near, of these whom life condemns

LADY WENDY:

He found himself hooked on an object, it's a woman he soon realized

DEREK:

In a second-thought flounder, when she chanced to look round her

Lady Wendy was truly surprised

LADY WENDY:

He thought that she'd come to his rescue

DEREK:

And she thought that he'd come to hers

DEREK *and* LADY WENDY:

Thus they both found new purpose, came back to the surface

And very soon they were sitting by the fireside, sipping liqueurs

CHORUS:

Well, well, the stories we could tell of folk who lose their nerve

Well, well, two idiots saved from hell

Who got what they deserved –

Each other

(*The* CHORUS *continues until the song ends.*)

As the song ends LADY WENDY *and* DEREK *are seen sipping liqueurs in her boudoir. A doorbell rings and* DEREK *slips out.*

LADY WENDY: (*She is a bit pissed as a newt*)

Oh jolly fine.

Oh jolly jolly fine.

Now naughty Wendy can mend her ways.

I'll buy him woollies from

Scotch House and pretend I

knittknitted them myself;

I'll inshure him for the Nissan

and we'll always be happy.

(*The* SINISTER MINISTER *enters.*)

SINISTER MINISTER: I'm in a frightful bind. The complete records of the club were taken from my briefcase this morning. We are all compromised and will be forced to flee.

LADY WENDY: (*Pissed and in love*) Oh Hugo, not now. I've met a working willy, for God's sake. Jolly Fine.

SINISTER MINISTER: If I don't find the thief before the bidding starts, it's the polo fields of South America for you and I, my dear.

LADY WENDY: Who did this dirty deed? Surely not your splendid little chum? Jolly Fine.

SINISTER MINISTER: 'Fraid so. The silly bisom must have had a brainstorm. Giddy up! Giddy up! I'm sure she bears no malice. I always thought she rather enjoyed chastising their various lordships and what have you.

LADY WENDY: Jolly Fine.

SINISTER MINISTER: Born to the task and no harm done, so to speak. Why, she positively sparkles as the governess of love. Are we doomed to become yet more tidbits at the breakfast table of the great unwashed?

LADY WENDY: Skates on, Hugo, or we'll all be down the lavvy.

SINISTER MINISTER: I am driven.

LADY WENDY: Jolly *Fine*! Fine!

(*'The Sinister Minister Theme' is heard.*)

DELILAH *is at her dressing-table, making up a parcel of two video-cassettes, a folder, a notebook and some square, flat, floppy-disc envelopes. She opens the folder and takes out a few stapled sheets with a polaroid photograph attached to the corner of one.*

DELILAH: Lord Singen Blue-tit, aged fifty-seven, life member. Video-reference 17B. Rating: seriously peculiar, highly damaging to international relations. Embarrassment factor: £250,000 plus. My god, it's blackmail. See page three for peccadillos. (*She turns to page three*) Oh, naughty Lord Blue-tit, that's a new one on me. (*She rifles through other files in the folder*) Christ, they're all here, and all the deals. Petro-dollars and Switzerland and everything. (*She starts making up the parcel*) I think I'm in serious trouble. If Sir Hugo catches me, we'll all be murdered in our beds.

Men. Bloody men have been after me since I was fourteen. And before that, the dirty buggers. Not all of them though;

some of them only wanted to look at me or be seen with me.
One lonely old buzzard bought me a Ferrari so we could drive from Amsterdam to Brussels for lovely meals.
They paid for my company and they were always good company, and some of them are my friends, but none of them will help me now.
The ones I call the lovers, however freaked out they are, only want to help themselves.
They say they like everything, but they don't really like anything, and all they want is more.
They couldn't help me now; not one of them; not in any way.
Not even the mesmerized ones, and certainly not the jack-the-lads. Nor the powerful ones or the weak ones, and definitely not the man in the street. What have I done?
I've taken this nest-egg, and it's hatching into an alligator.
What am I going to do?
I wish I had a bloody friend.
(DELILAH *exits.*)

The CHORUS *sings 'Sally'.*

'Sally'

CHORUS:

Sally, Sally
don't ever wander
away from the alley and me
Sally, Sally
pride of our alley
you're more than the whole
world to me
When skies are grey
you'll be crying
When skies are blue
you'll be smiling, smiling

Enter DELILAH. *She's on the street and is desperate. She sings 'Looking for Harry', narrowly avoiding the* SINISTER MINISTER.

'Looking for Harry'

DELILAH:

Looking for Harry, looking for Harry, looking for Harry
Looking for Harry
Looking for Harry, have you seen him around?
The minute I find him, I'm going to unwind him
It's time to remind him not to put me behind him
Looking for Harry, perhaps he's gone underground
Loving him is going to be beautiful, beautiful, all night long
(Loving him is going to be) beautiful, beautiful, all night long

Checking for Charlie, checking for Charlie, checking for Charlie
Checking for Charlie, oh wherever's he been?
Been trying to bell him, in order to tell him
The minute I smell him I'm going to unshell him
Checking for Charlie, since he's been off the scene
Loving him is going to be beautiful, beautiful, all night long
Loving him is going to be beautiful, beautiful, all night long

All night long, all night long, all night long, all night long . . .

(DELILAH *exits, as* PC HONEY *enters. Then* SIMPSON *enters from the opposite side of the stage.*)

PC HONEY: (*Cocky beyond his experience*) Oy, you!

SIMPSON: Who, me?

PC HONEY: Yes, you. I know you. You're up to no good. What are you up to?

SIMPSON: I'm up to my earholes with soppy policemen. Piss off!

PC HONEY: I could have you: I could have you under Section 43 for loitering, littering, fouling, obstructing, and stealing the pavement; vagrancy, public affray and ABH to my eyesight. I'm old Bill! I can fit you right up!

SIMPSON: (*Now angry, confronts* PC HONEY) Not on a one-to-one basis you couldn't, sonny Jim. Now, fuck off or else I'll spank you!

(PC HONEY *makes a frightened exit.*)

SIMPSON *sings 'A Bit of Kit'.*

'A Bit of Kit'

SIMPSON:

I want a three-piece suit in black gaberdine, with a three-button jacket and a notch lapel
With a boxy back, French shoulder and a zig-zag raised seam that you do so well
18-inch bottom trouser with a 2-inch cuff; no taper, no flare: just parallel

Wing-tipped brogues, fisherman's warms, red longjohns chillproof vest of the snuggest fit
Second-hand Turnbull and Asser sea-island cotton shirt with no collar attached to it
Black Burberry trenchcoat, white silk scarf, no groins or kettle, that should complete my kit
And then I want to live in a conversation area

(SIMPSON *has just finished 'A Bit of Kit' when he spots* DELILAH. *He is pleased to see her.*)

It's you.

DELILAH: (*Not pleased to see Mr Mouthy*) It's you.

SIMPSON: It's you!

DELILAH: It's you . . .

SIMPSON: I own this land, as far as the eye can see, and one of these days it's going to be yours.

DELILAH: Everyone was put on earth for a purpose.

SIMPSON: (*He can see she's got troubles*) One night when the moon is full, you'll look out of your window and see a man on a white horse up on yonder ridge. That'll be me. Do you hold a library card?

(*She smiles.*)

Do you know the work of Horace McCoy? Eric Ambler?
(*She shakes her head.*)
Burl Ives?

DELILAH: When the bluebird sings and the lemonade springs on the big rock candy mountain.

SIMPSON: Well, they don't make them like that any more.

DELILAH: This could be bigger than both of us.
(*Music starts for 'Game On'.*)

'Game On'

SIMPSON:
Although I nearly broke my neck trying to break the ice
I think you're very nice
Let's go and have a drink, what d'you think?
Throw six and go to jail

DELILAH:
Although I've met a mouthy man or two before
You've got the highest score, I'm sure
I don't mind if I do have a drink with you or two
Game on

SIMPSON:
I'll try and pull the verbal back a bit in case
Your earache threatens our relationship
As a master crook I found out I'm a div
So now I make a meagre living as a spiv
It's all Jekyll

DELILAH:
I'm not sure if I want to tell you much about me recently
It's hard to put it decently
I used to do exotic dances, but nowadays I concentrate on taking stupid chances
(*She clutches her parcel.*)

SIMPSON:
I feel like there's a bond with you

DELILAH:
I'm getting very fond of you

SIMPSON:

It's good to correspond with you

DELILAH:

I wish I could abscond with you

SIMPSON *and* DELILAH:

Well well, ah well, well well
Well well, ah well, well well
Well well, ah well, well well
Well well, ah well, well well

SIMPSON:

Welcome to my quarters, pull a bed up
Sorry it's a tip, it's furnished from a skip
I rarely entertain here; usually I roll back pissed, get blocked and fall straight into kip
More fool me

DELILAH:

I'm a very nosy person, can I look?
God, you've got a lot of books, haven't you?
I'm not much of a reader myself
Literature rather left me on the shelf
As it were, I mean was

SIMPSON:

The days it isn't going well, I tell the world to
go to hell and slam up here with Edgar Allen Poe
or Ruth Rendell, and I feel better straight away
That's all I can say about books

DELILAH:

When I wake up and this is all gone
Or something spoils it, and it was all bollocks anyway
It will still be good

SIMPSON *and* DELILAH:

Well well, ah well, well well
Well well, ah well, well well
Well well, ah well, well well
Well well, ah well, well well

(They have just finished 'Game On', fallen asleep and they are lovers. It is morning.)

DELILAH: (*Putting the parcel in front of her, she speaks in a worldly way*) I've got something to tell you. I stole this off a very rich trick. It's worth a lot of money, but now I've met you, somebody to love, and I don't want it any more. I can't throw it in the river cos it's my life insurance, and I can't give it back cos they'll still come after me. What am I going to do?

SIMPSON: (*He totally accepts what she has just said*) You keep out of the way and I'll give it back. As far as life insurance is concerned, you're with me now, and I'm the Abbey National.

DELILAH: It's too dangerous. If they see you, they'll kill you.

SIMPSON: They won't see me; I went to boarding school.

DELILAH: I took it from a house in Chelsea.

SIMPSON: I know Cheyne Walk like the back of my hand.

SIMPSON *meets* BILLY *in the pub. He is about to return the parcel.*

BILLY: (*Lifts his pint in a straight glass*) The higher up you go, the less alarms there are. I used to be able to climb a drainpipe faster than it could fall off the wall.

SIMPSON: (*Lifts his pint in straight glass and puts the parcel on the table*) I want to go in and out, quiet as a mouse, and leave it on the carpet.

BILLY: When I was in Wandsworth there were three blind burglars in there. Not related; all pros though. At least, they were till they got caught.

SIMPSON: Well, I'm not getting caught.

BILLY: In the old days, when I was at it, they would phone up and ask for Spider. If I didn't fancy it, I'd say, 'No, this is Billy', and they'd leave it out. If I was up for it, I'd meet 'em in here for a shant, and they wouldn't let you out of their sight till the job done. Then you got driven home.

SIMPSON: Nobody's driving me home.

BILLY: I'll wait up the road for you, with the motor.

SIMPSON: It's a shame you've knocked it on the head. If I knew a few more like you, I would never have left the profession.

BILLY: It's hard to find the right people.

(BILLY *and* SIMPSON *sing 'The Right People'.*)

'The Right People'

BILLY:

People think it's easy being a crook
But I got done for everything I took
There's people who could keep you out of shtook
But you've had it if you don't know where to look

SIMPSON:

People think it's easy being a thief
But all my major tickles come to grief
The only way your talent is revealed
Is working with the top men in their field

BILLY *and* SIMPSON:

It's hard to find the right people
It's hard to find the right people
It's hard to find the right people

People think you've only got to ask
And turn up with your crowbar and your mask
'Good morning, I'm a burglar, what's the haps?'
But you've had it if you haven't met the chaps

It's hard to find the right people
It's hard to find the right people
It's hard to find the right people

BYLINE BROWNE *is interviewing the* SINISTER MINISTER, *who is giving a reluctant interview. He is worried. The rumours are spreading.*

BYLINE BROWNE: Can you tell me sir, why Lord Haversack has taken a sudden holiday in Tuscany, and are you preparing your resignation?

SINISTER MINISTER: Members of the Cabinet and their whereabouts are no concern of mine, and are subject to D Notice. I have absolutely no intention of seeking pastures new as long as I enjoy the confidence of my prime minister.

BYLINE BROWNE: What do you know of Delilah Dolittle?

SINISTER MINISTER: My supper club has an annual open

evening. I believe she was a guest of the Under Secretary of Over-Development. You can't print any of this, you know. If you think Sir Humphrey would forsake his peerage for a nine-day wonder in the *Bugle*, you're up the Congo, you tawdry little hack.

BYLINE BROWNE: I'm a freelance and I'm sticking up your arse, you slimy bastard.

In the process of trying to return the parcel SIMPSON *sets off the alarm. He throws the parcel to* BILLY. *It comes on top for* SIMPSON.
PC HONEY *arrests him.*
'On Top on Top on Top' is sung.

'On Top on Top on Top'

SIMPSON:

On top on top on top, (PC HONEY *joins in*) your life of crime must stop
The odd lot are upon you, (PC HONEY *joins in*) and though you're on your toes
Let's have some lights, (PC HONEY *joins in*) you're bang to rights
Well bugger me and stone the crows: would you suppose?

Police oppose the suspect's bail, (MAGISTRATE *joins in*) Magistrate him straight to jail
Have a lay-down on remand, (WARDER *joins in*) don't get out of order
Or you will get a reprimand (WARDER *joins in*) from the prison warder

Comes the day they hear your case, (MAGISTRATE *joins in*) that fat old windbag knows your face
Although you've got a high-class brief, (MAGISTRATE *joins in*) you got no chance of winning
No more shants or tickles thief, (MAGISTRATE *joins in*) you're going to get a skinning

The magistrate sits there and scowls
and sends the frighteners up your bowels

SIMPSON *and* MAGISTRATE:

I find you guilty of this charge
And may it prove your nemesis
The world's not safe while you're at large
Unlawfully entering premises.

(BILLY *joins in*) Newgate's under the Bailey, and Brixton's where you've been
(PC HONEY *joins in*) You're starting at a half-stretch in Wormwood Scrubs
(MAGISTRATE *joins in*) So don't make a fuss when you're chained to the bus
(WARDEN *joins in*) Or we'll have to be obscene

Inside inside inside, (BILLY *joins in*) a hard man and his pride
Forget about your memory, (BILLY *joins in*) and as the main gates close
Don't lose your starch (BILLY *joins in*) beneath the arch
The rest of you will decompose, if your bottle goes

Hello choirboy, welcome back, (WARDER *joins in*) hold your hand out for a smack
Notorious hardbitten villain, (WARDER *joins in*) vicious and violent and fast
If his arse-hole was half an inch wider, (WARDER *joins in*) he'd go to the top of the class

Remove your watch and ring and clothes, (WARDER *joins in*) and give 'em here, we're keeping those
Bend over prisoner, for a spin, (WARDER *joins in*) I'll see what I can find
In case you're trying to smuggle in (WARDER *joins in*) a gun up your behind

(BILLY *joins in*) Banged up in your peter, got everything you need?
(PC HONEY *joins in*) You clench your fist, recidivist
(MAGISTRATE *joins in*) And we'll tuck you up and we'll fuck you up
(WARDER *joins in*) And we'll make your kidneys bleed

BILLY: On reception there's always a con lurking about. Sweeping or something. He'll bring things in for you, but it's always on the fifties. He keeps half. It's always on the fifties. If you're lending tobacco baroning burn they call it, it's on the fifties every week. That used to be the reason a lot of geezers went over the wall in the old days. They'd build up such a huge debt with the barons, they could never repay it, but if you're out for twenty-four hours it clears your slate and men would rather lose their remission than have that hanging over 'em. Me, I never smoked, so I was always a rich man.
SIMPSON: Last Sunday I had two joints, a glass of Chivas and some serious acid. What's happened to that young woman?
BILLY: I don't know. I'll try and find out. Is there anything you need?
SIMPSON: Yes.
(*Final chorus of 'On Top On Top On Top'*.)

DELILAH *is seen, lost and alone. She enters spot-lit and sings one line of 'Looking For Harry', unaccompanied.*

ACT TWO

BYLINE BROWNE *enters, speaking on the Vodaphone.*

BYLINE BROWNE: I'm the only one who knows the full story. You would have sacked me months ago. Don't talk to me like that, you wanker. Listen, you prat, it doesn't hinge on the tart. You know who I'm talking about – I'm not obsessed, you berk – I've been trained for this mission. Bollocks!

(*He puts away the phone and addresses the audience.*)

Six months later. I've got to tell you, I've had it up to the eyeballs with this caper. My major source is on the missing list. Her dodgy boyfriend's doing bird for trying to break into Lady Wendy's house in Chelsea and my right-hand man won't tell me a bloody thing about who pays his bloody wages.

(BILLY *appears.*)

What's going on?

BILLY: This I do not know. On my life, stand on me.

BYLINE BROWNE: Bollocks. The Wagmore Club is closed up tight and all activities appear to have ceased. The Sinister Minister is clinging to office in spite of a mass of early retirements in the lower echelons.

Where is she?

BILLY: Nobody knows where she is, and lots of people are looking for her.

BYLINE BROWNE: I can't crack this story without her. You know I'll see her all right. I've been reduced to steaming letters and following secretaries about all over the bloody Home Counties. I might as well hand in my ration-book. I can't go near the news desk; they think I've lost my grip. We've got to find her.

BILLY: Yes, guv. I'm going to Streatham this afternoon to have a dig about. (*He leaves.*)

BYLINE BROWNE: Bloody Streatham., Have I been reduced to this? Where did I go wrong? Is this my mid-life crisis? Streatham.

Well, it's not all gloom.

The music starts for 'England's Glory'.

'England's Glory'

There are jewels in the crown of England's glory
And every jewel shines a thousand ways

Frankie Howerd, Noël Coward and garden gnomes
Frankie Vaughan, Kenneth Horne and Sherlock Holmes
Monty Biggles and Old King Cole, in the pink or on the
dole
Oliver Twist and Long John Silver, Captain Cook and
Nellie Dean
Enid Blyton, Gilbert Harding, Malcolm Sargent, Graham
Greene

All the jewels in the crown of England's glory
Too numerous to mention but a few
And every one could tell a different story
And show old England's glory something new

Nice bit of kipper and Jack the Ripper and Upton Park
Gracie, Cilla and Maxie Miller, Petula Clark
Winkles, woodbines, walnut whips, Vera Lynn and
Stafford Cripps
Lady Chatterley, Muffin the Mule, Winston Churchill,
Robin Hood
Beatrix Potter, Baden-Powell, Beecham's powders,
Yorkshire pud

With
Billy Bunter, Jane Austen, Ray Ellington, George
Formby
Billy Fury, Little Tich, Uncle Mac, Mr Pastry and all
Uncle Mac, Mr Pastry and all

All the jewels in the crown of England's glory
Too numerous to mention but a few
And every one could tell a different story
And show old England's glory something new

All the jewels in the crown of England's glory
Too numerous to mention but a few
And every one could tell a different story
And show old England's glory something new

Somerset Maugham, top of the form, and the boy's brigade
(England's glory)
Mortimer Wheeler, Christine Keeler and the Board of Trade
(England's glory)
Henry Cooper, Wakey-wakey, England's labour
Standard Vanguard, spotted dick, England's workers
(England's glory)
(BYLINE BROWNE *exits.*)

GEORGE *and* REENIE *are leaning over the parapet at Westminster Embankment, throwing the last of their lunches to the sea-gulls.*

GEORGE: I was thinking of bringing the Morris in on Friday. We could pop out of London.

REENIE: Ooh George, d'you think we really ought? Tom and Lance'll be expecting their bit of supper.

GEORGE: Yes, and Maud will have the fish-cakes waiting, but we can't hold back our feelings for ever. (*He throws his last crumbs*) Let's throw caution to the winds.

REENIE: (*Throws her last crumbs and snuggles up*) The die is cast. (*They part surreptitiously.*)

We are on a dark street.

DELILAH *emerges from the gloom to smile at a passing car. It fails to stop and she sinks back into the shadows. A second car approaches, she steps out and smiles. She sees the car stop in the wings and scampers after it.*

BILLY *is visiting* SIMPSON *in prison. He places teas, Cokes, biscuits and chocolate on the table.* SIMPSON *scoffs the lot.*

BILLY: If you can't do the time
Don't do the crime.

SIMPSON: I'm surprised they let you in here.

BILLY: Here's the new P. D. James . . . Did I tell you about the time that Cohen fried the corn beef's hat, all covered in batter, and filled it up with chips?

SIMPSON: Have you found her yet? Where is she? I haven't heard nothing all this time.

BILLY: (*Puts the book down*) Not yet, and I ain't the only one who's looking. There's all kinds of people after her, including my employer. She's a naughty girl.

SIMPSON: Can your man help her?

BILLY: He thinks she can help him. I think she might have gone south.

SIMPSON: What, awayday?

BILLY: Streatham.

SIMPSON: Oh, Streatham. Say no more.

BILLY: If I find her, I'll tell Browney. He won't stitch her up.

SIMPSON: Find her for me, Bill.

Rhythms begin for 'All Those Who Say OK'. SIMPSON *is alone in his prison cell, listening.*

'All Those Who Say OK'

VOICES:

All those who say OK, say OK. OK?
All those who say OK, say OK.

Philosophy philosophy philosophy philosophy
Philosophy philosophy philosophy philosophy
Philosophy philosophy philosophy philosophy
Philosophy philosophy philosophy philosophy

What makes you think I think you think
I think you think I think you can think?
What makes you think I think you think
I think you think I think you can think?

For instance: For instance.

For instance: For instance.
Exactly.

SIMPSON:

I see you're reading a book,
Have you got to page one yet?
You're so stupid you don't know you're not
Asking about what you don't know about
And now you're confused as well
If you've got any sense at all
Which I doubt.
You're so negative that you've become a transparency
Which nobody wishes to view

You're so lazy that it's a wonder you
Haven't been castigated by the less fortunate
For wasting your god-given talents.
Well now you have a sucker
Can you tell me the way straight on please?
Please will you tell me
One thing you can do with a pencil?

You're so selfish that if you had anything to say
You'd keep it to yourself.
You couldn't hold the floor
If you was lying on it.
Can you spell your name forwards?
If you were going somewhere
Would you start from here?
How many beans make five, sucker?

(*As the song ends* SIMPSON *is very dejected.*)

DELILAH *steps out of a phone box. She has been decorating it with little stickers.* PC HONEY *appears.*

PC HONEY: (*Trying to be fatherly*) And what are you up to, then?

DELILAH: I was making a transfer charge call. Would you like to make a transfer charge call?

PC HONEY: (*Embarrassed but still earnest*) I'm on duty madam, and under the Street Offences Act of 1963, I might have to take you in charge.

(DELILAH *walks towards him seductively*. PC HONEY *backs away from her, flustered*.)

DELILAH: I'm already in charge little man, and you're impersonating a police officer. Come here.

PC HONEY: (*He has lost control of the situation*) Not now, madam, I'm wanted at the station.

(PC HONEY *makes a backwards exit, with* DELILAH *almost pulling the buttons off his tunic*.)

REENIE *is on the telephone*.

REENIE: Is that you, George? I've only got a minute. Are you still on for this evening? Oh, good. I'll be free as soon as his horrible nibs has finished recording his broadcast. Queen Boadicea at five o'clock? Oh. lovely. Hmmm. You too.

(*The* SINISTER MINISTER *enters and* REENIE *goes official*.)

Yes, yes, very good sir, you'll have it in front of you by six o'clock. Goodbye.

SINISTER MINISTER: (*Removing his make-up bib*) Are we on auto-cue?

REENIE: (*Her sarcasm no longer subtle*) Unless you've got a better idea, minister.

(*The TV lights are switched on and the* SINISTER MINISTER *faces the camera*.)

SINISTER MINISTER: (*He clears his throat; he is moving his hands very anxiously*) Are we ready? Are my hands in shot? Are we doing cutaways?

(*He is given the go-ahead*.)

Good evening. I'm addressing you tonight on a matter of great importance. Over the past few weeks, nay months, certain opposition members and journalists of the gutter press have implied, nay insinuated, that irregularities of an unspeakable nature have been taking place in the corridors of office and its environs. Let me hereby put paid to these rumours once for all, and scotch these awful slurs.

True, some very junior parliamentarians are now paying dear for what I can only find it in my heart to describe as youthful folly: the chamber-pot on the gilded spire, so to speak.

Giddy up! Must we pillory these poor souls and tar others with the same brush, or can we not as citizens of this fair land leave the stone unturned? I appeal not only to your good sense, for was it not indeed we who introduced fair play? Or shall we wilfully smite away the bails from the crease of the mother of democracies? I thank you for your time, and God bless you.

(*The arc lights go down and the* SINISTER MINISTER *turns to* REENIE.)

Haven't they found that bloody tart yet?

REENIE: (*She is doing her hair and make-up*) I'm going back to the pool on Monday.

SINISTER MINISTER: (*Oblivious to her statement, clutching his ulcers*) Phone the agency. I want more operatives. The PM's having kittens and the Cabinet is hanging by a thread.

REENIE: (*Putting on her coat and scarf*) I'm leaving you to wallow in your own droppings, minister.

SINISTER MINISTER: (*Realizing he's almost alone*) We weren't hurting anybody. We were only being naughty in the Edwardian manner: the kiss of the lash and a dash of hellfire. So to speak. Lie!

REENIE: With blackmail and coercion, you loathsome ninny. What about that poor girl? If you ever get your hands on her, I dread to think what you'll do.

SINISTER MINISTER: I'll forgive and forget handsomely. Just twenty minutes with the shredder and the Bahamas will be her oyster.

(*'The Sinister Minister Theme' begins.*)

REENIE:

Your goose is cooked you nincompoop and I for one will
gladly watch you hanging by the bollocks in the mire
So as you reap what you have sown
Remember this, you're all alone
The frying-pan has tipped you in the fire

SINISTER MINISTER: (*Dropping to his knees as* REENIE *departs*)

Oh pardon me for I have sinned
The deepest pangs of true remorse
Have cut my very spirit to the core

(*He realizes she's gone and gets up again alone. He is suddenly sorry and like an honest child.*)

I promise not to hurt that girl
I'll just destroy the evidence
And I promise I won't do it any more

BYLINE *and* PC HONEY *are outside the ministry.* BYLINE *is showing* PC HONEY *a photograph.*

PC HONEY: I can only see a pair of legs, sir. Have you tried missing persons?

BYLINE: Have you never seen these legs popping up the Minister's steps while you've stood here shivering all night on guard-duty? There's a good drink in it for you.

PC HONEY: (*Bristles*) Are you trying to tamper with the long arm of the law, sir? I might have to caution you. We're not allowed to take inducements. How much did you have in mind?

BYLINE: I was thinking in terms of a long 'un. So you do know this person?

PC HONEY: I can get that for doing a football match, sir. I don't know what you're talking about.

BYLINE BROWNE *spies on* REENIE. GEORGE *and* REENIE *meet in the country.*
They have been followed by BYLINE *who photographs them with a growing sense of regret and a telephoto lens.*

'George and Reenie'

BYLINE BROWNE:

There's a tryst after work, civil servants from Whitehall
In a lay-by some miles from the busy A3
Twixt George from accounts and Reenie from planning
Having each told their spouses they'd be home after tea
'It's been ages,' said George as he parked up the motor
'I've fancied you since you was in personnel'
'Feeling's mutual,' said Reen, as they clambered through hedgerows
'I'm ever so glad you came out of your shell'

Soon they stood face to face in a field of some acres
Quite nervous but glad that they'd taken this risk
No longer spring chickens but game as two good 'uns
Despite the constructions of George's slipped disc
They were thwarted at first for a spot to canoodle
For the nettles were tall and the brambles were thick
The minute he spread out his green tartan car-rug
She said, 'It's quarter past six, George, we'll have to be quick'

Evening sun lit the scene for the two would-be sweethearts
Lo, the earth truly moved at their very first kiss
For their nuptial couch, it transpired, was a quagmire
Whence cow-pasties squelched and foul cases didst hiss
'Oh my god,' shouted George as the slime tugged his elbows
And he felt his libido sink slowly from sight
With a murmur of pity she leant back on her haunches
Adding to his discomfort with the top of her tights

As she searched for her purse midst a halo of midges
And he groped for his keys and his specs in the swamp
George and Reenie experienced some serious seconds
Cos they'd only set out for a bit of a romp
'See you Monday,' said George as he dropped her in Clapham
Though the pong was alarming he smiled as he spoke
'Ta-ta, Georgie,' said Reen and she patted his bottom
'Though you're hardly Paul Newman, you're my type of bloke'

BYLINE *hands binoculars and outdoor gear to* BILLY.

BYLINE: Well, that's it. I'm finished. I've just been following his secretary about all over the home counties. Coitus interruptus on the Guildford by-pass. Not even one dirty little paragraph. It's time to shut up shop.

BILLY: All is not lost. I have just this minute ascertained the whereabouts of the said young woman: she's in a right old state: on her last knockings you might say.

BYLINE: Is she ready to talk?

BILLY: I believe she is.

BYLINE: Lead on MacDuff.

(They depart.)

We hear the CHORUS *singing 'Sally'.*

DELILAH *emerges from the gloom on a dark street. She sees someone coming and, with a look of fear, she ducks back into the alley. The* SINISTER MINISTER *prowls by but fails to see her.*

DELILAH: It's only a matter of time. I can't live like this much longer. That bastard's killed my lover and he won't rest until he's done for me. I wish I had a mum and dad.

(She sings 'On The Game'.)

'On The Game'

You made me what I am
It's not your fault you messed me around
You had your reasons
Take the can back, take the can back, take the can back
Or kick the bucket
And screw me in turn

For years the same, and no love came, you're on the game
I call your name, you're in the frame, you're on the game

I'm doing this because of that
It couldn't be avoided, more's the pity
Knowing why ain't knowing nothing
Take the can back, take the can back, take the can back
Or kick the bucket
Sympathy is pimpathy

Love, limp and lame, oh what a shame, you're on the game
I call your name, you're in the frame, you're on the game

Take the can back, take the can back, take the can back
Or kick the bucket
And screw me in turn

For years the same, and no love came, you're on the game
I call your name, you're in the frame, you're on the game
Love limp and lame, oh what a shame, you're on the game
I call your name, you're in the frame, you're on the game

Take the can back, take the can back, take the can back
Or kick the bucket

We hear 'On The Game' end. BILLY *shows* BYLINE BROWNE *where* DELILAH *stands soliciting.*

BYLINE BROWNE: I'm here to find out what makes you tick.

DELILAH: (*Jumps with fear*) Oh my God, what do you bloody want?

BYLINE BROWNE: I've been trying to find you for months. What's brought you out into the open?

DELILAH: (*Clutches her arm*) You're working for Sir Hugo Sinister and I'll be murdered in my bed.

BYLINE BROWNE: For what it's worth, I'm still on the *Bugle*. My offer still stands. What have you got on him?

DELILAH: I had the works. All the juice on all the members of the Wagmore – videos and gory details. But it's disappeared and so has the brave man who tried to help me. I think they've killed him.

BYLINE BROWNE: Who, your barrow-boy? Don't be daft. He's in the nick. He slipped back into his old ways.

DELILAH: For me. He was helping me. He was going to put it back.

BYLINE BROWNE: If he put it back, why is all this panic going on? The Chiltern Hundreds are like Waterloo Station. You keep your head down, lassie, and I'll see what I can do. Billy says your spiv's put you on a VO for Sunday, at the Scrubs.

DELILAH: You're a toff. I won't forget this.

PC HONEY *strolls up and they exit in opposite directions. The* SINISTER MINISTER *enters and produces a photograph. He shows the photograph to* PC HONEY, *who stands rigidly to attention in the presence of government.*

SINISTER MINISTER: This is a matter of high security. Have you seen this woman? The nation awaits your answer.

PC HONEY: Yes, sir, only a moment ago sir. I can't see her legs but I'm sure it's her sir. She was heading north in the company of a suspicious character.

SINISTER MINISTER: This is top secret. Tell no one. You must find her and bring her to me. Your country will be very grateful.

PC HONEY: (*Still to attention*) Very grateful, sir?

SINISTER MINISTER: The CID are crying out for men like you. I have a certain influence. I expect results.

PC HONEY: Yes sir, thank you sir.

(*The* SINISTER MINISTER *exits.* PC HONEY *sings 'PC Honey'.*)

'PC Honey'

PC HONEY:

I'm only nineteen, I'm a little bit green
I've yet to be corrupted by the frightful things I've seen
With my measured pace and bright young face
I only want to make the world a safer place

PC Honey to the rescue . . . PC Honey up a drainpipe
PC Honey on the zebra . . . PC Honey's on patrol

I've done the course and I've joined the force
I'm a brave upstanding bobby full of keen resource
Make me use my feet, keep me on the street
So I know everybody up and down my beat

PC Honey to the rescue . . . PC Honey up a drainpipe
PC Honey on the zebra . . . PC Honey's on patrol

For every crook who faces me
And every raging mob
A copper's what I chose to be
It's all part of the job

As you steal or poach, beware my soft approach
With nothing but a truncheon and a talking brooch
I'm a figure of fun who doesn't need a gun
And you're going round the nick, my son

PC Honey to the rescue . . . PC Honey up a drainpipe
PC Honey on the zebra . . . PC Honey's on patrol

DELILAH *visits* SIMPSON *in prison. She is heavily disguised. He does not recognize her at first. They sing 'It's You'.*

'It's You'

SIMPSON:
It's you
DELILAH:
It's you
SIMPSON:
It's you
DELILAH:
It's you
SIMPSON *and* DELILAH:
It's you

I've been wondering all the time if –
There's so many things that I've –

It's been all I could do just to –
I really honestly thought that –

I can hardly believe that this is –
It's such a relief to know that –

SIMPSON:
No, go on

DELILAH:
No, go on

SIMPSON:
No, go on

SIMPSON *and* DELILAH:
It's so good to see you again
I've been thinking about you for every minute of every day
Are you OK? I love you
No, after you
I love you
No, after you

SIMPSON:
It's you

DELILAH:
It's you

SIMPSON:
It's you

DELILAH:
It's you

SIMPSON *and* DELILAH:
It's you

(*'It's You' Ends.* DELILAH *and* SIMPSON *face each other across the table piled high with food and cups of tea, which* SIMPSON *ignores.*)

DELILAH: I've bought some books. Horace Whatsit.

SIMPSON: You been OK? Did Billy find you?

DELILAH: Yes, I've been in the suburbs. That reporter spoke to me. I thought you were dead. What happened?

SIMPSON: I was half-way up the wall when everything went off. I didn't see the camera. I only just had time to dump the gear.

DELILAH: What, in the river?

SIMPSON: I'll tell you when I come home. Billy says my place has been turned over more than once since I've been away.

DELILAH: I'm so glad you're all right.
SIMPSON: Keep safe for a little bit longer, darling, and look after that white horse I told you about.

The SINISTER MINISTER *is buttonholed by* BYLINE BROWNE *outside the ministry.*

BYLINE BROWNE: Minister? Browne, DPI. I'd like a minute, off the record.
SINISTER MINISTER: You're a little man with a dirty face and a dirty tongue. Now bugger off.
BYLINE BROWNE: Listen, you berk peer. I know where she is and I know what you're looking for.
SINISTER MINISTER: Oh really? Then why haven't you crucified me in your filthy rag, you oik?
BYLINE BROWNE: We want to do a deal. You can witness the destruction of the material in exchange for her safety and your resignation.
SINISTER MINISTER: And what do you get out of it?
BYLINE BROWNE: A job on the *Independent.*
SINISTER MINISTER: I don't believe you've got it! Officer! Arrest this man. He's trying to blackmail me!
PC HONEY: (*He salutes*) Yes, Mr X.
(*To* BYLINE BROWNE)
You, come with me. You're fucking nicked.
(BYLINE *is taken into custody.*)

BILLY *hands* SIMPSON *the parcel.*

BILLY: A friend is somebody, you go round their house and say 'Look after this for me' and you give 'em a brown paper parcel. You come back six months later and they haven't looked inside it.
(*They sing 'The Right People' reprise.*)

SIMPSON:
It was very educational in custody
BILLY:
One often hears it's only education that one needs
SIMPSON:
One's just left university with one's degree

BILLY:

That this will set one up in life for all one's future deeds

SIMPSON:

One's results were quite sensational: one got A and B

BILLY:

One has to work one's toe-nails off in order to succeed

SIMPSON:

In thieving and perversity from one through three

BILLY:

And one agreed

SIMPSON:

It was rehabilitational, believe you me – I mean one.

BILLY:

One's told that fortune only ever smiles on ones who wait

SIMPSON:

Equipped to face adversity, they set one free

BILLY:

Although one's every effort seems designed to be too late

SIMPSON:

And after one's probational, the world might see

BILLY:

One's oft assured that diligence provides a flowing plate

SIMPSON:

In criminal diversity, a Ph.D

BILLY:

And one says 'great!'

BILLY *and* SIMPSON:

If you're on your best behaviour doing bird
They reduce your prison sentence by a third
And the only thing you want when you get out
Is to link up with the chaps who've got the clout . . .
It's hard to find the right people
It's hard to find the right people . . .

(*They exit, still singing, arms linked, and well geed.*)

DELILAH *enters on her way to meet* SIMPSON. *The* SINISTER MINISTER *suddenly appears.*

SINISTER MINISTER: My dear –

(DELILAH *screams and runs into the arms of* PC HONEY.)

PC HONEY: (*To the* SINISTER MINISTER) I saw that! I'm arresting you for harrassment alarm and distress. Stop!

(*The* SINISTER MINISTER *tries to flee, but encounters* SIMPSON *and* BILLY, *still singing 'The Right People'. They hand him over to* PC HONEY.)

PC HONEY: I'm going to take down your particulars.

(BILLY *and* PC HONEY *march the* SINISTER MINISTER *off, and* SIMPSON *and* DELILAH *sing 'Love is All' reprise, holding the parcel between them.*)

'Love is All'

SIMPSON:

I've just this minute got out of the boob
I wonder, could you show me to the tube?

DELILAH:

The understanding is it's just because
The underground is where it always was.

SIMPSON:

Come to my arms

DELILAH:

Seeing it's you

SIMPSON:

My new-found love

DELILAH:

I might as well

SIMPSON:

As spirits soar

DELILAH:

You're all I've got

SIMPSON:

I'm worlds above

DELILAH:

So what the hell

SIMPSON:

And while we pledge

DELILAH:

If you want me

SIMPSON:

Our hearts be true

DELILAH:

To hold you, dear

SIMPSON:

This new-found dream

DELILAH:

Stop talking bullshit

SIMPSON:

Of me and you

DELILAH:

In my ear

SIMPSON *and* DELILAH:

Cos love is all
Love is all.

BYLINE BROWNE *is in the dock. He sings 'The Courtroom reprise.'*

BYLINE:

I formerly came here to mock
And laugh at the pure poppycock
So it's come as a bit of a shock
To find that it's me in the dock
To find that it's me in the dock
To find that it's me in the dock

(*The* MAGISTRATE *harangues* BYLINE.)

MAGISTRATE: (*Heavy rhythm plays*) You and your ilk, Mr Browne, are the true bane of our society. You feed on the weak unfortunates who stray into temptation.
You pander to puerile curiosity and peddle your perverted truths with no thought of the pain you cause, the families you break up, or the lives you destroy. You turn human foible into hideous fables.
Your lust for sensation drives you beyond the pale. You create reputations in order to ruin them, then you greedily devour the corpses of your victims. You hunt your prey like

members of a death squad.
You show no mercy as you pillage the privacy of innocent and guilty alike. You cheapen and coarsen the quality of life with your hollow smut. I hate you. Do you understand?

BYLINE BROWNE: I just want to say I'm very sorry and and I'll never do it again.

(The last chorus of 'The Courtroom Song' is heard as the SINISTER MINISTER *enters with* PC HONEY, *and* SIMPSON *and* DELILAH *enter with the parcel.*
'Love is All' chorus swells, as BYLINE BROWNE *shouts out)*

Oh no, it ain't!

*(*BYLINE BROWNE *sets fire to the parcel. As it begins to glow, the lights come down and the cast come forward, singing 'Love is All'. They gradually become silhouetted against the fire. The audience begins to sing 'Love is All'.*
The song ends. Everybody fucks off.

BYLINE BROWNE *introduces the cast and tells the end of their stories, and introduces the musicians and the singers.*

'Riding the Outskirts of Fantasy'

Little tests and odd requests, who loves who loves who the best?
Little tasks, no questions asked, the traitor is at last unmasked
Little ploys, search and destroy, who brings who brings who more joy?
Little snipes and frequent gripes, taken in by all the hype

We're riding the outskirts of fantasy
We're riding, we're riding, we ride
We're hiding our loss of identity
We're keeping our secrets inside

Little tricks with walking sticks, who gives who gives who more kicks?

Little smiles and wily wiles, got your name down on our files

We're riding . . .

BYLINE:

I have done this and that
I have been here and there
I had tasted the fruit
Of the coco de mer
I've devoted myself
To a life without care
And when all's said and done
I've done more than my share

Little games, we name no names, who lost who lost who more aims?
Little snares caught unawares, the cupboard underneath the stairs

We're riding . . .